W9-AGD-644

THE SPIDER

For Emma,
who, like the spider, is not an insect

Text and illustrations copyright © 2015 by Elise Gravel
Copyright for the French edition: Elise Gravel and Les éditions de la courte échelle inc., 2015
Paperback edition published in 2016 by Tundra Books, an imprint of Penguin Random House Canada
Young Readers, a Penguin Random House Company

All rights reserved. The use of any part of this publication reproduced, transmitted in any form or by any
means, electronic, mechanical, photocopying, recording, or otherwise, or stored in a retrieval system,
without the prior written consent of the publisher—or, in case of photocopying or other reprographic
copying, a licence from the Canadian Copyright Licensing Agency—is an infringement of the copyright law.

Library and Archives Canada Cataloguing in Publication

Gravel, Elise
[Araignée. English]
        The spider / Elise Gravel.

(Disgusting critters)
Translation of: L'araignée.
Originally published by Tundra Books in 2015.
ISBN 978-1-101-91854-8 (paperback)

        I. Spiders--Juvenile literature. I. Title. II. Title: Araignée.
English III. Series: Gravel, Élise. Disgusting critters.

QL458.4.G7213 2016   j595.4'4   C2015-906951-3

Published simultaneously in the United States of America by Tundra Books of Northern New York,
an imprint of Penguin Random House Canada Young Readers, a Penguin Random House Company

Library of Congress Control Number: 2014941839

English edition edited by Samantha Swenson
Designed by Elise Gravel and Tundra Books
The artwork in this book was rendered digitally
Printed and bound in China

www.penguinrandomhouse.ca

9 10   23 22 21

Penguin
Random House
tundra | TUNDRA BOOKS

Elise Gravel

THE SPIDER

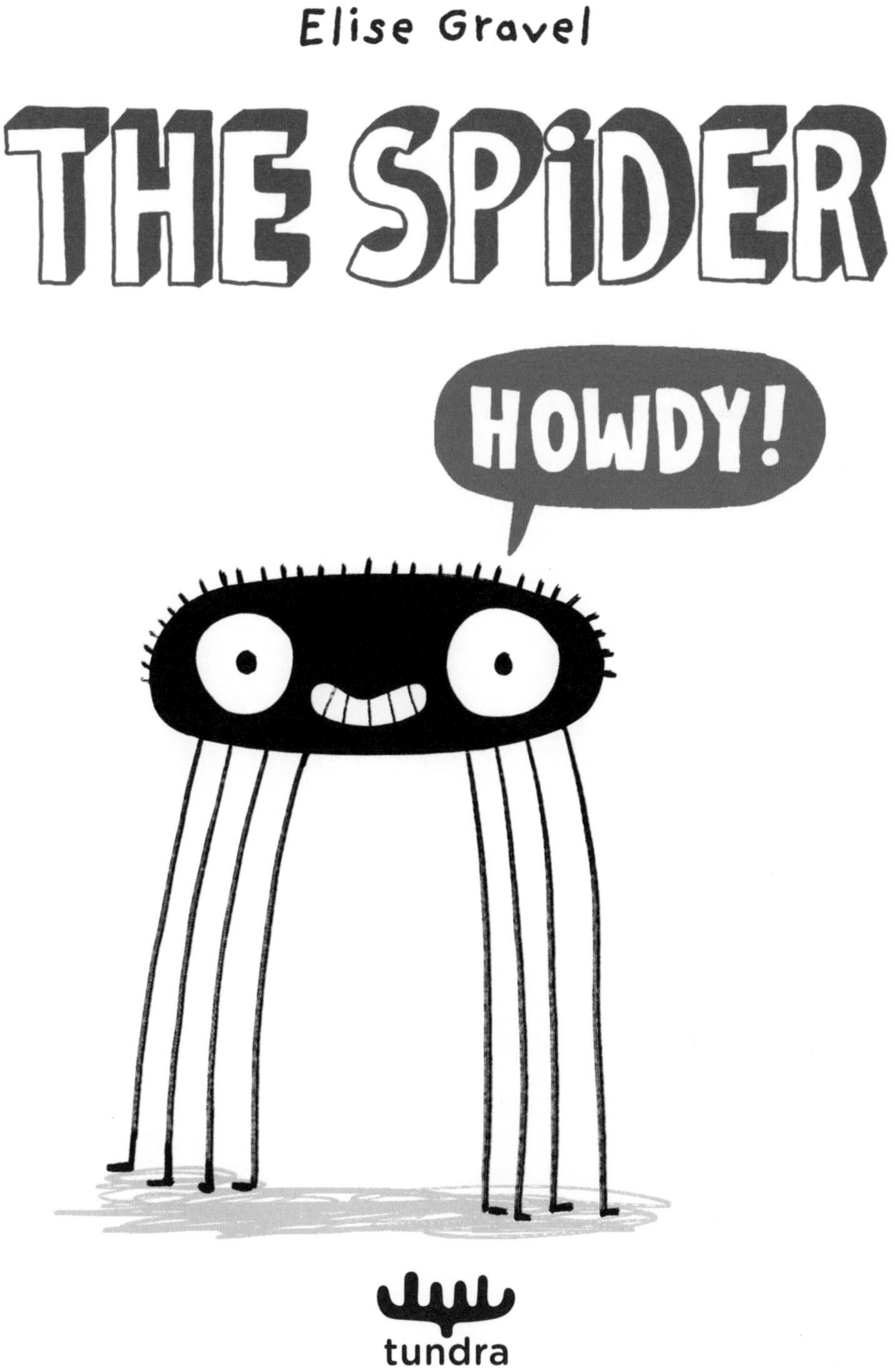
HOWDY!

tundra

Ladies and gentlemen, please welcome
your friend

THE SPiDER.

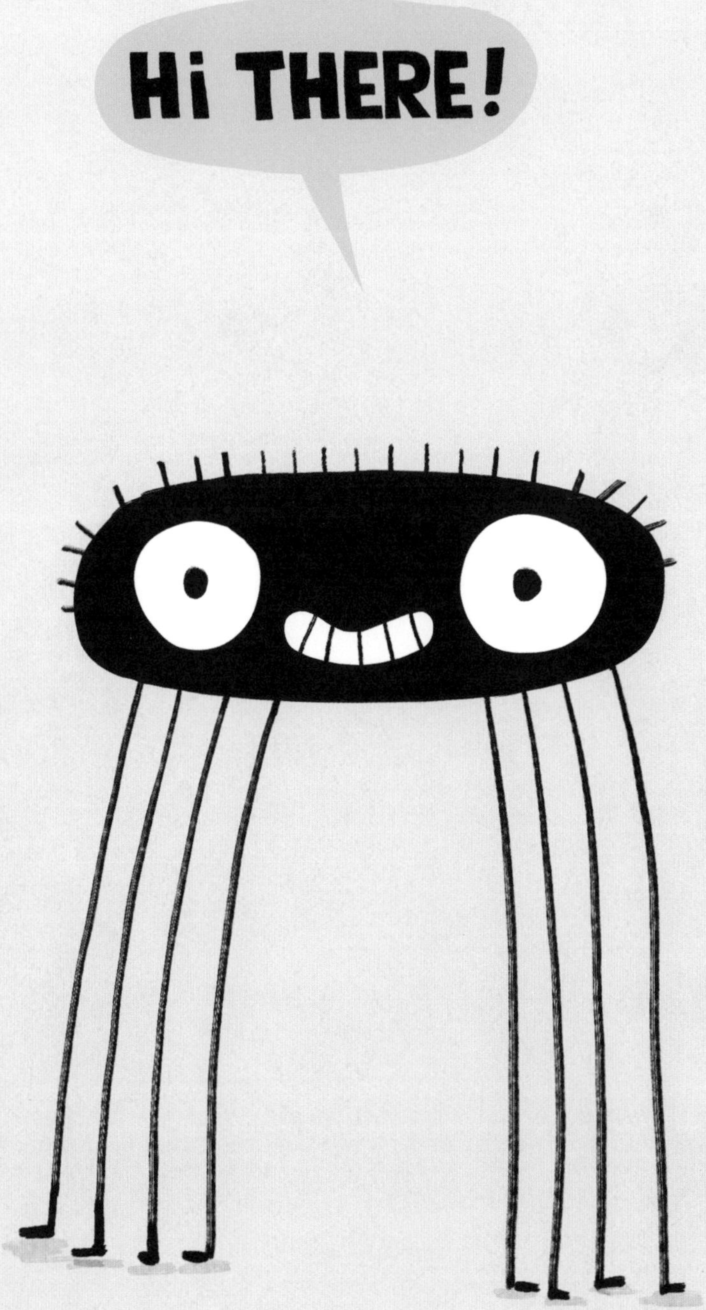
Hi THERE!

There are over 40,000 species of spiders. They can live in almost any environment:

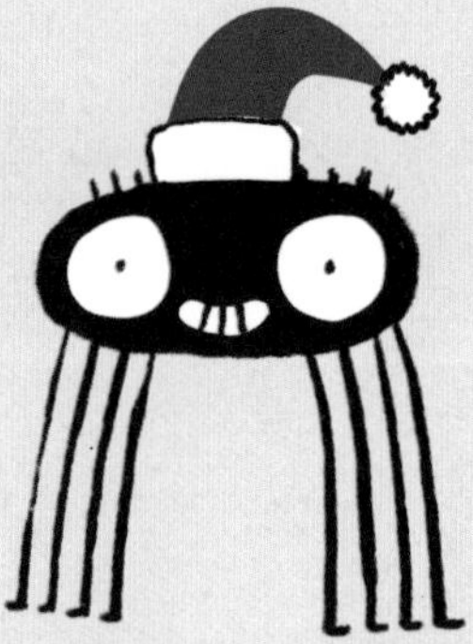

In cold climates

In warm climates

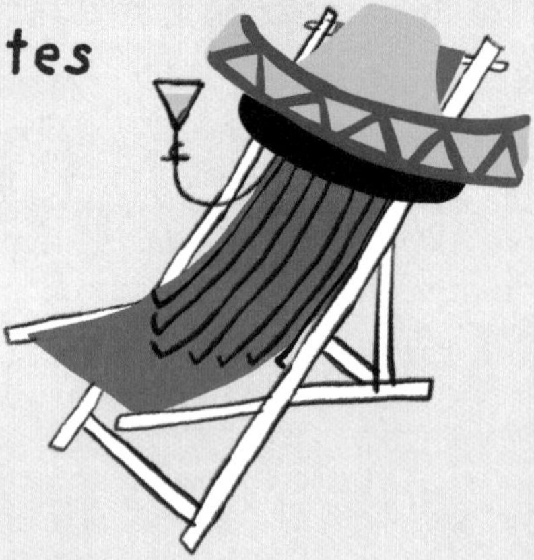

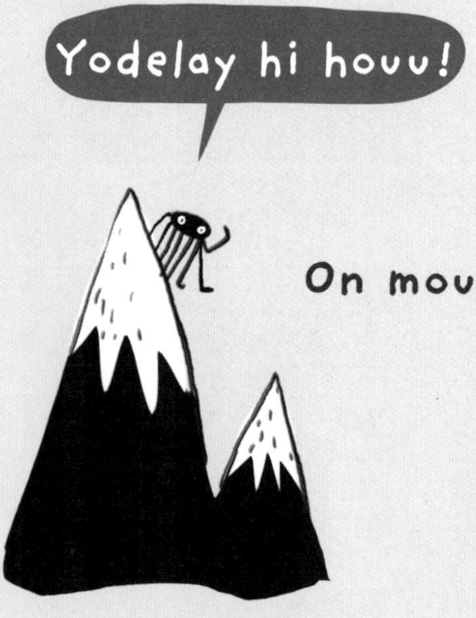
Yodelay hi houu!

On mountaintops

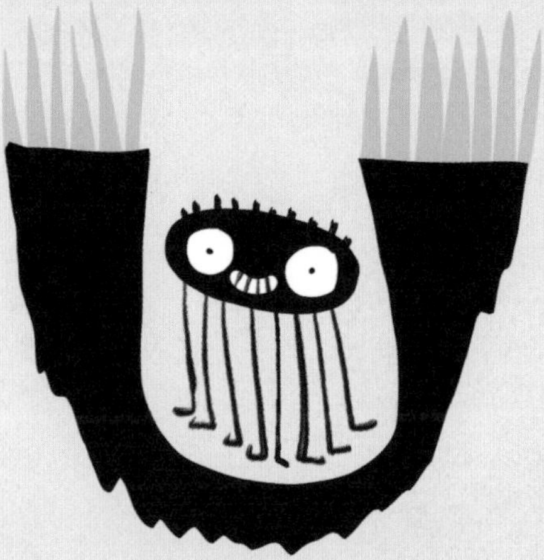

Underground

Underwater

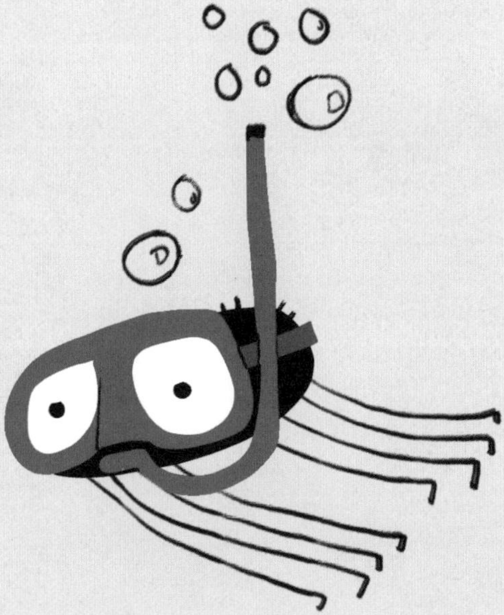

. . . But not in outer space.

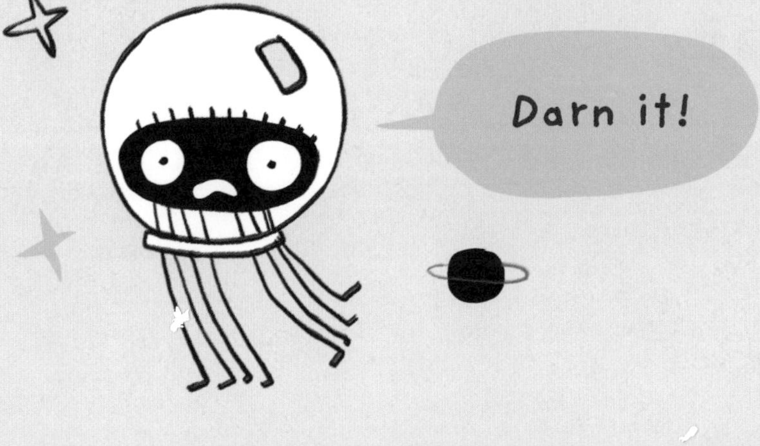
Darn it!

Since she has eight legs, the spider is not considered an

INSECT.

Insects only have six legs.

Maybe not, but I'm so pretty in princess shoes.

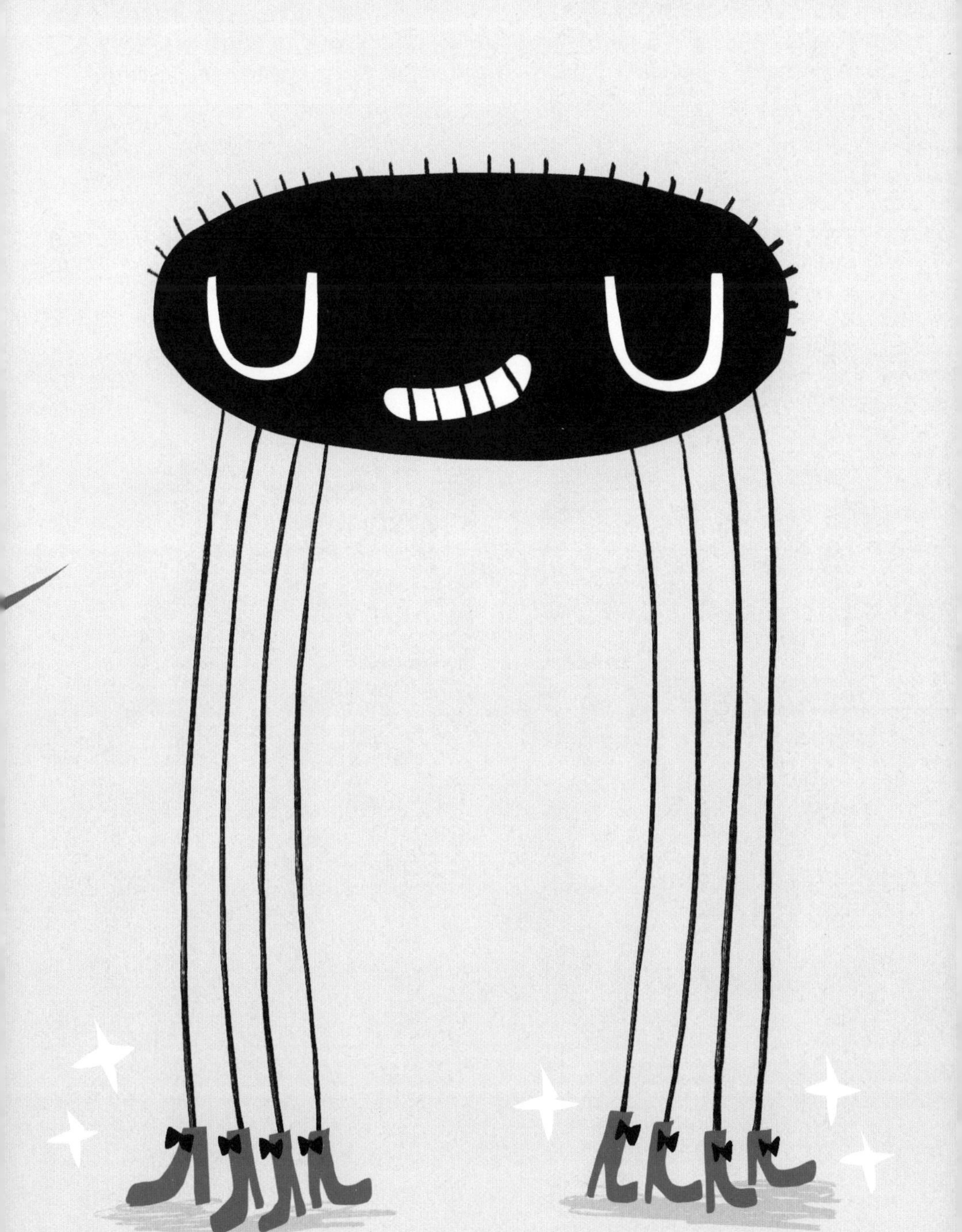

Most spiders have poisonous fangs in their mouths and

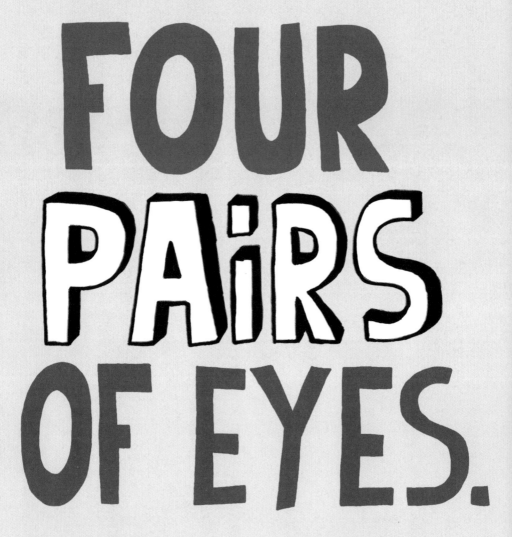

FOUR PAiRS OF EYES.

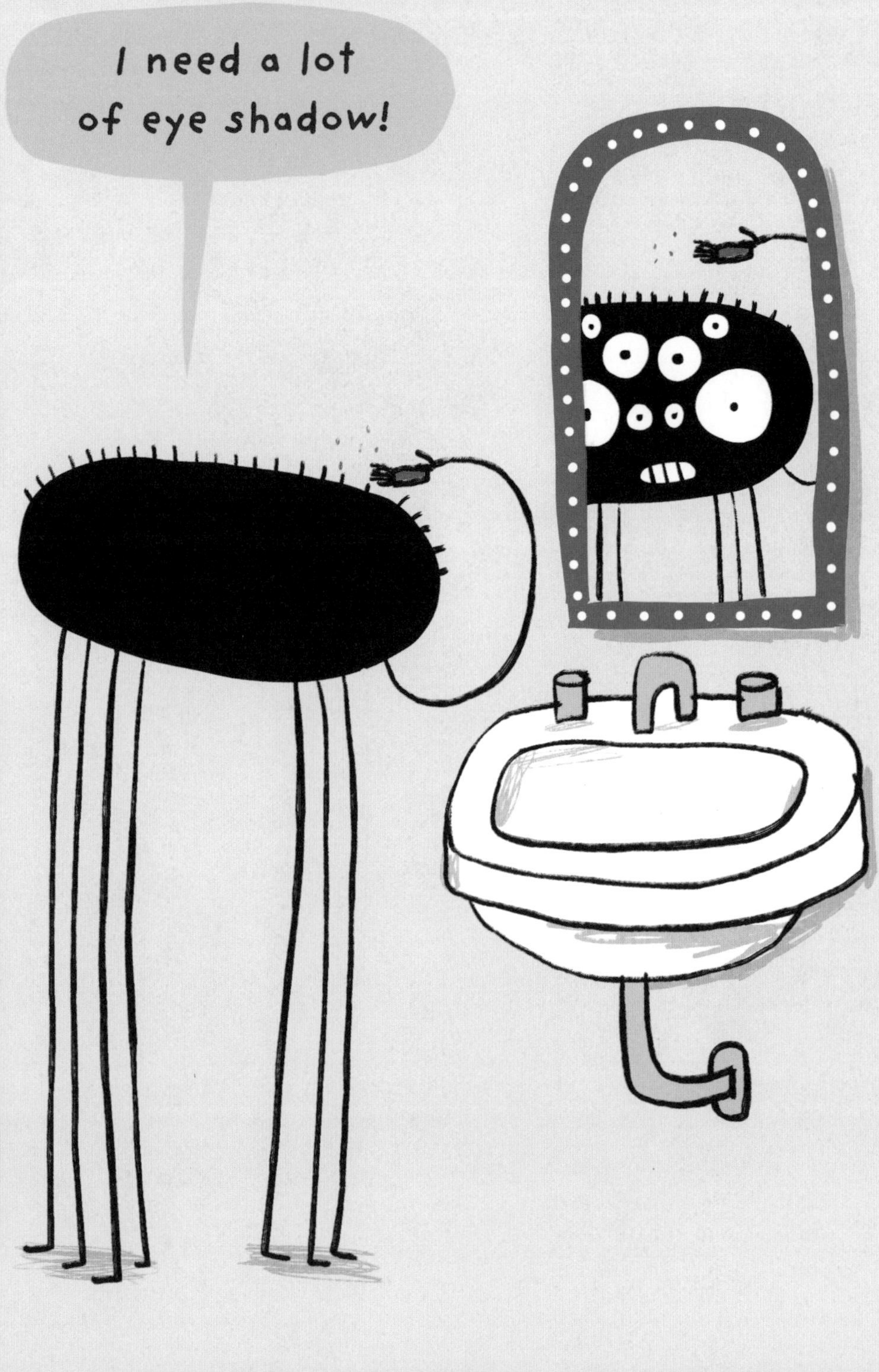
I need a lot of eye shadow!

Spiders produce

SiLK

with their abdomens.

Their silk can be used
for many things:

to build webs

ooOYOYOOO
OOOOOOO!

as a means of
transportation

to protect their eggs

to create webs that trap air so they can breathe underwater.

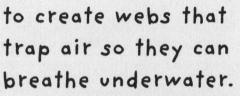

We also make really handsome ties.

Spiders mostly eat insects. They have many different ways of catching their prey: some use a sticky net as a trap, others jump on their prey and some catch their prey with a

LASSO.

YEEHAW!

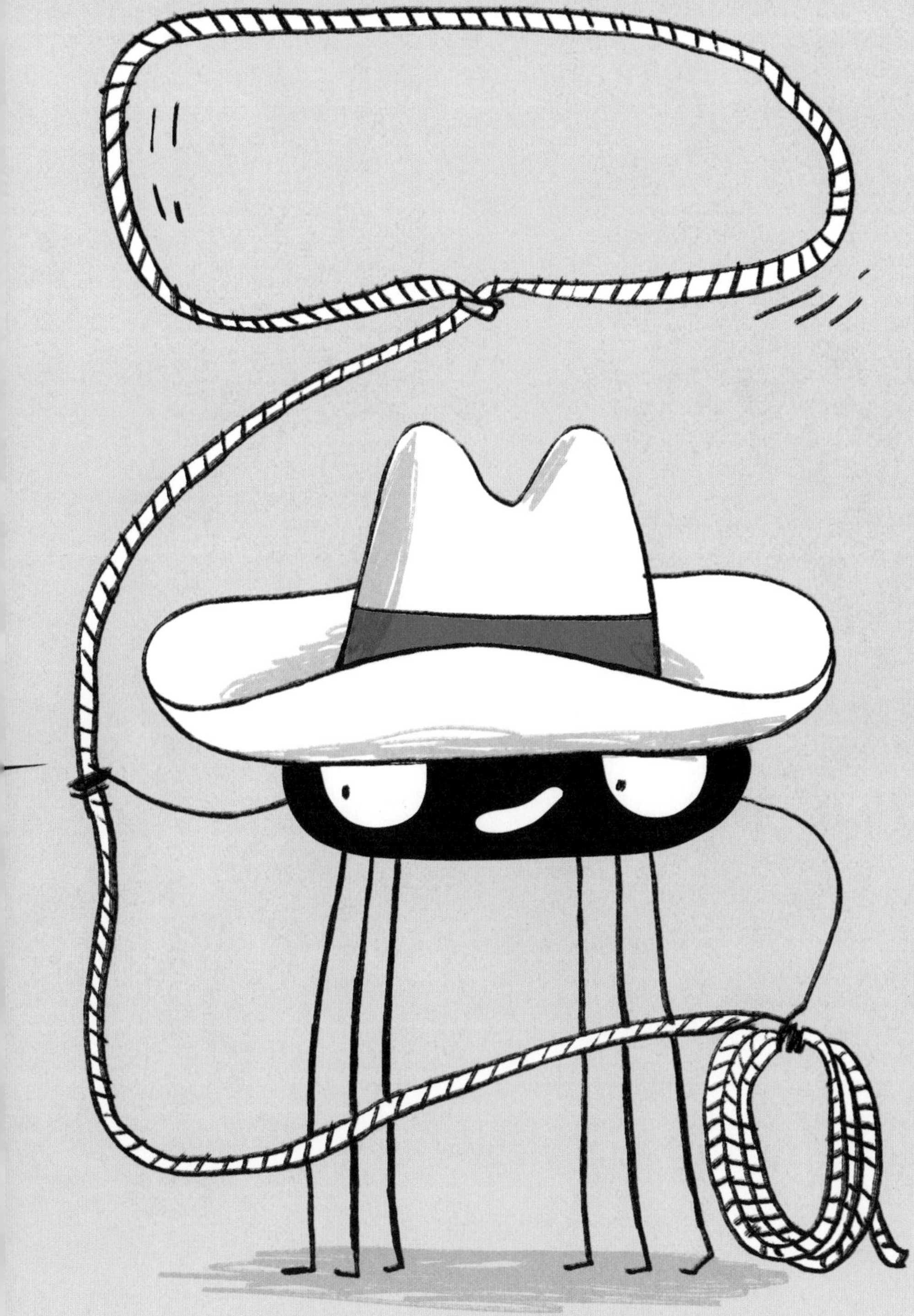

Some spiders even

MiMiC

their prey to make it easier to sneak up on them.

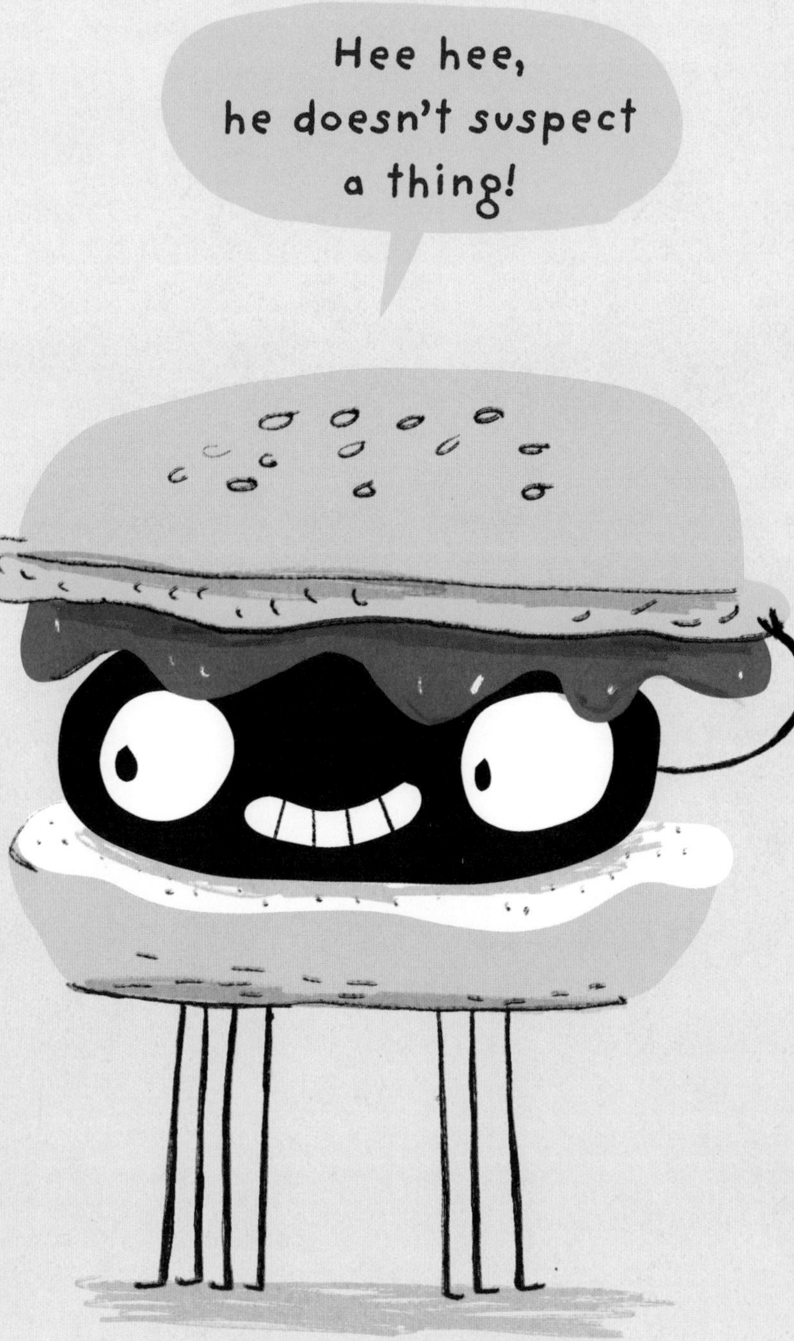
Hee hee, he doesn't suspect a thing!

In many spider species, the

is bigger than the

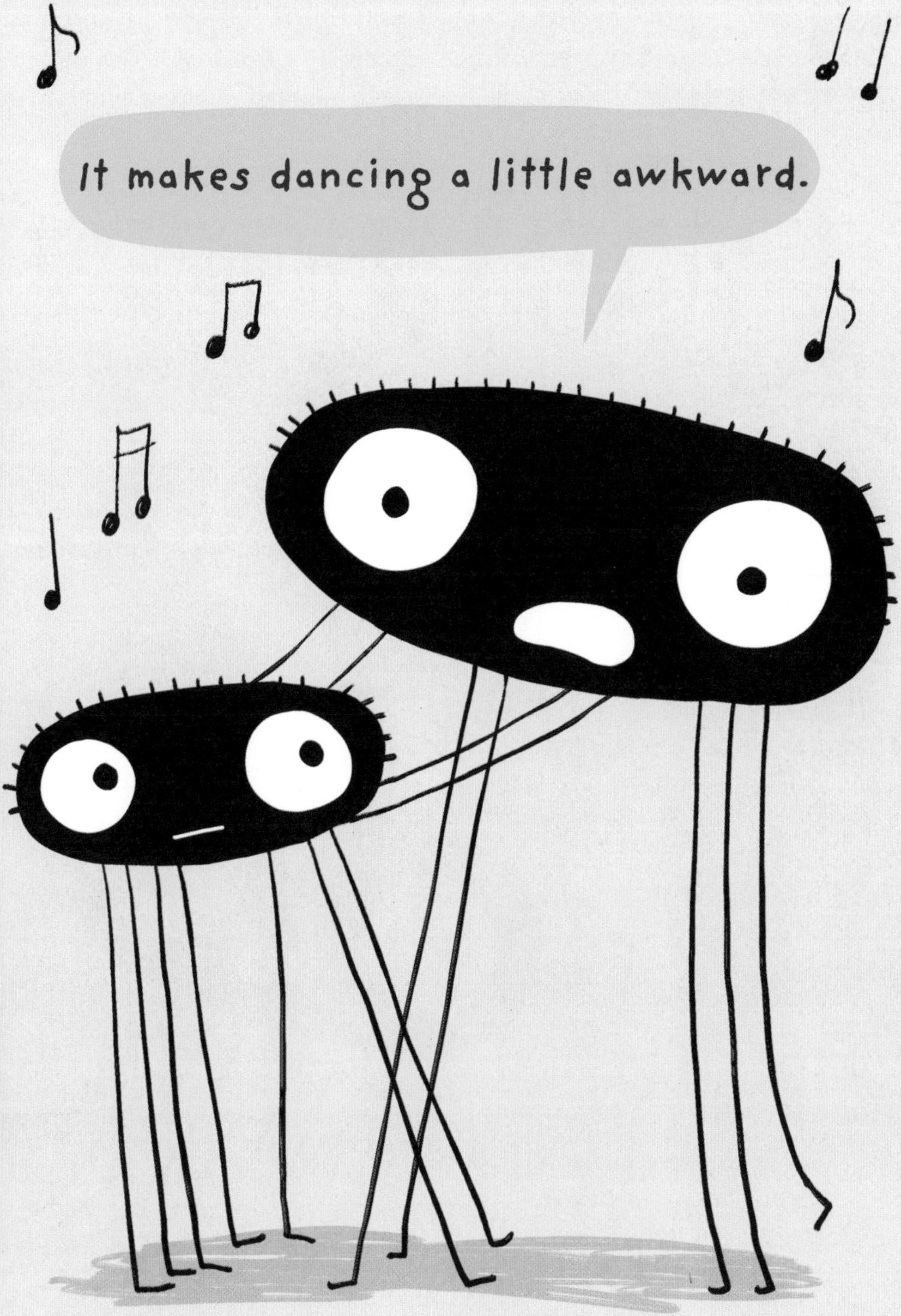
It makes dancing a little awkward.

After some spiders mate, the female spider will

EAT THE MALE.

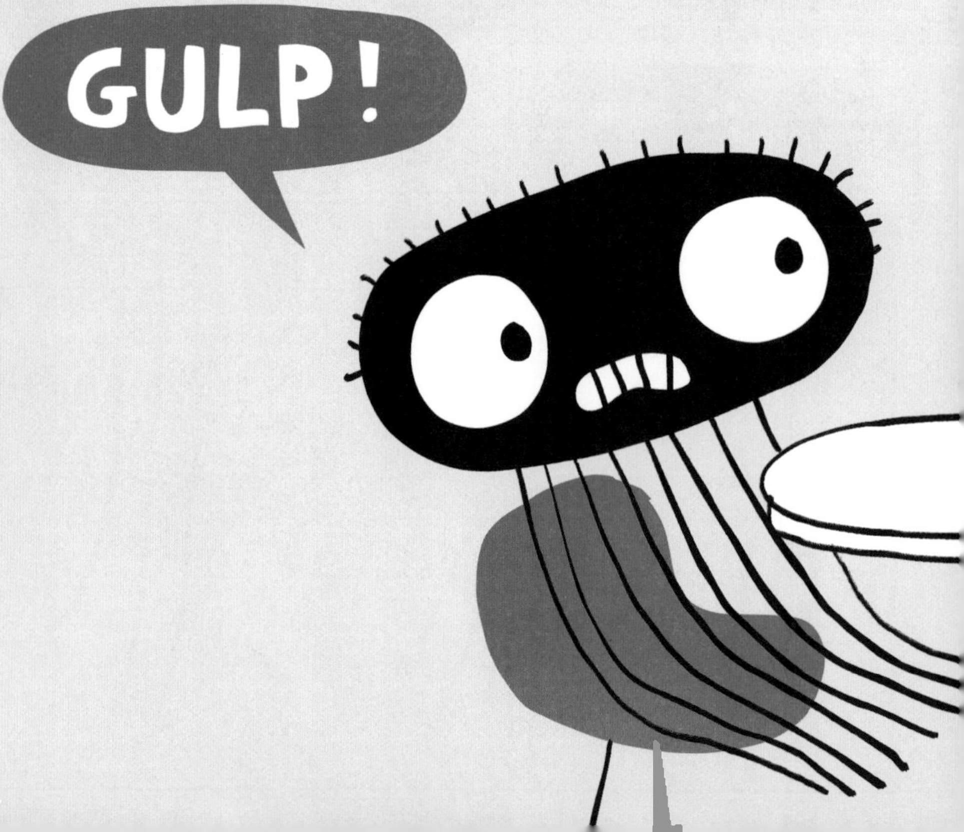
GULP!

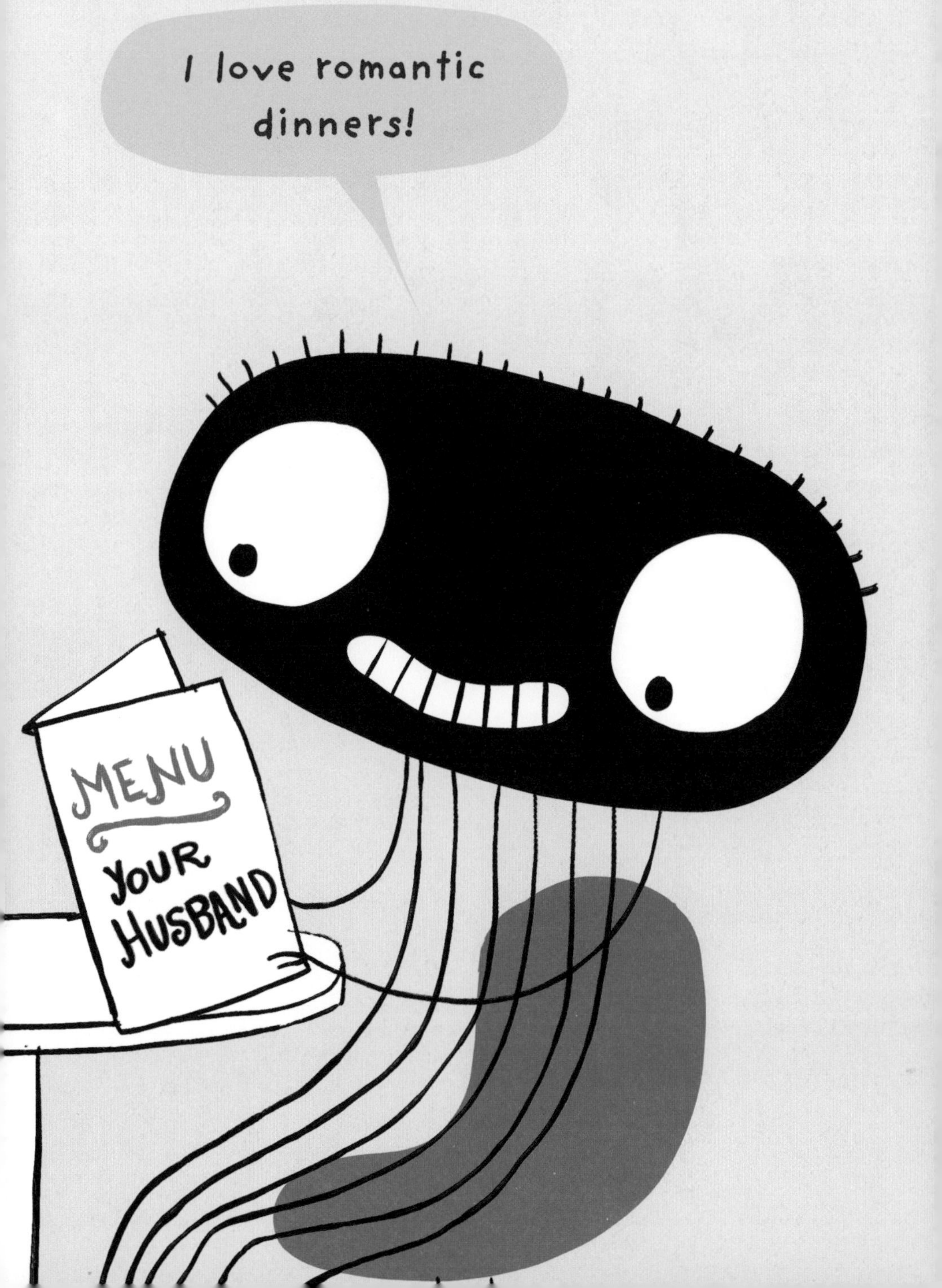
I love romantic dinners!
MENU
YOUR HUSBAND

The female spider can lay up to a thousand

EGGS.

She wraps them up in her silk and carries them around with her.

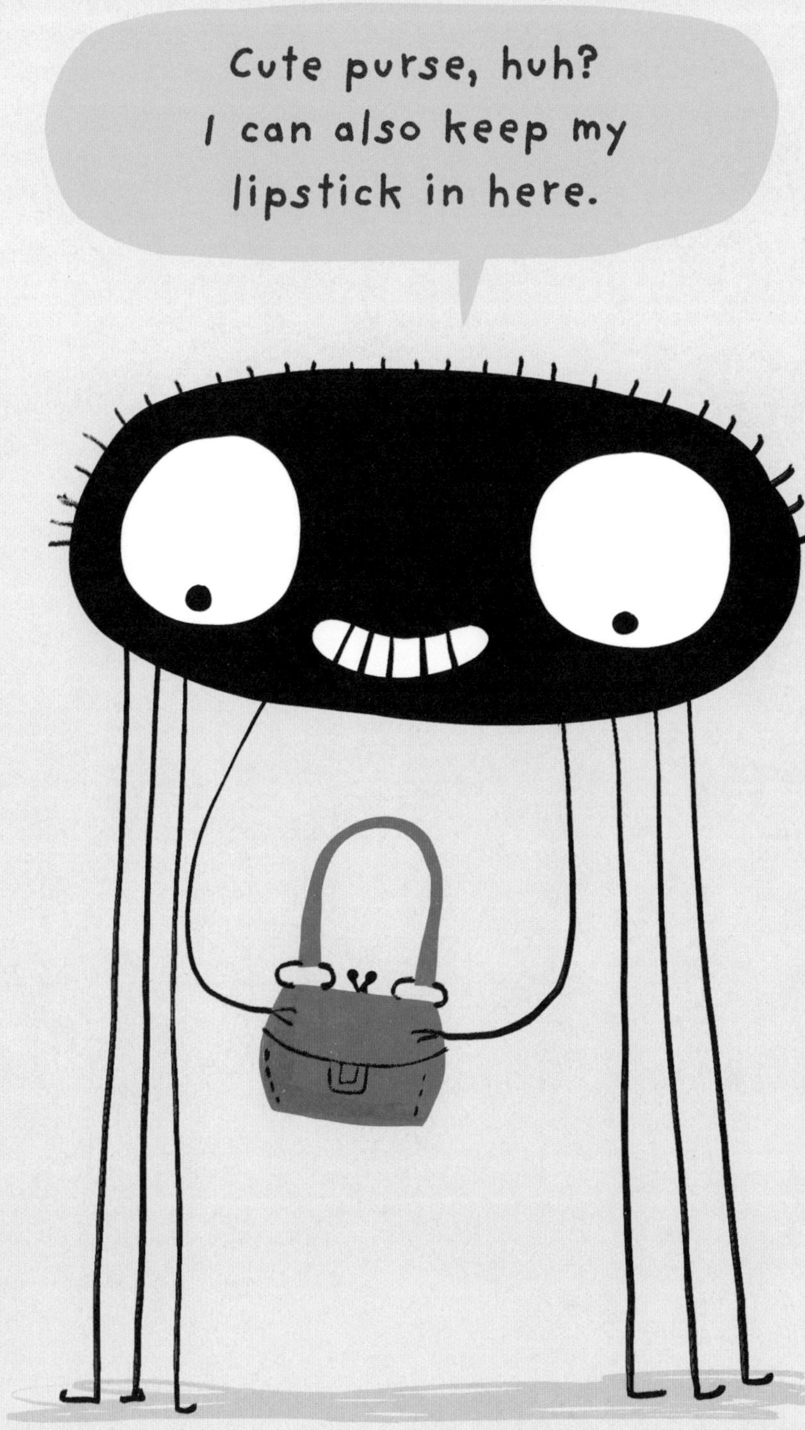
Cute purse, huh?
I can also keep my
lipstick in here.

Some mothers carry the baby spiders **ON THEIR BACKS** until the babies are old enough to **DEFEND** themselves.

Are we there yet?

Are we there yet?

Are we there yet?

People are often afraid of spiders, but most spiders are

NOT DANGEROUS

to humans. In fact, spiders have much more reason to be scared of us!

EEEEEEEEEK!

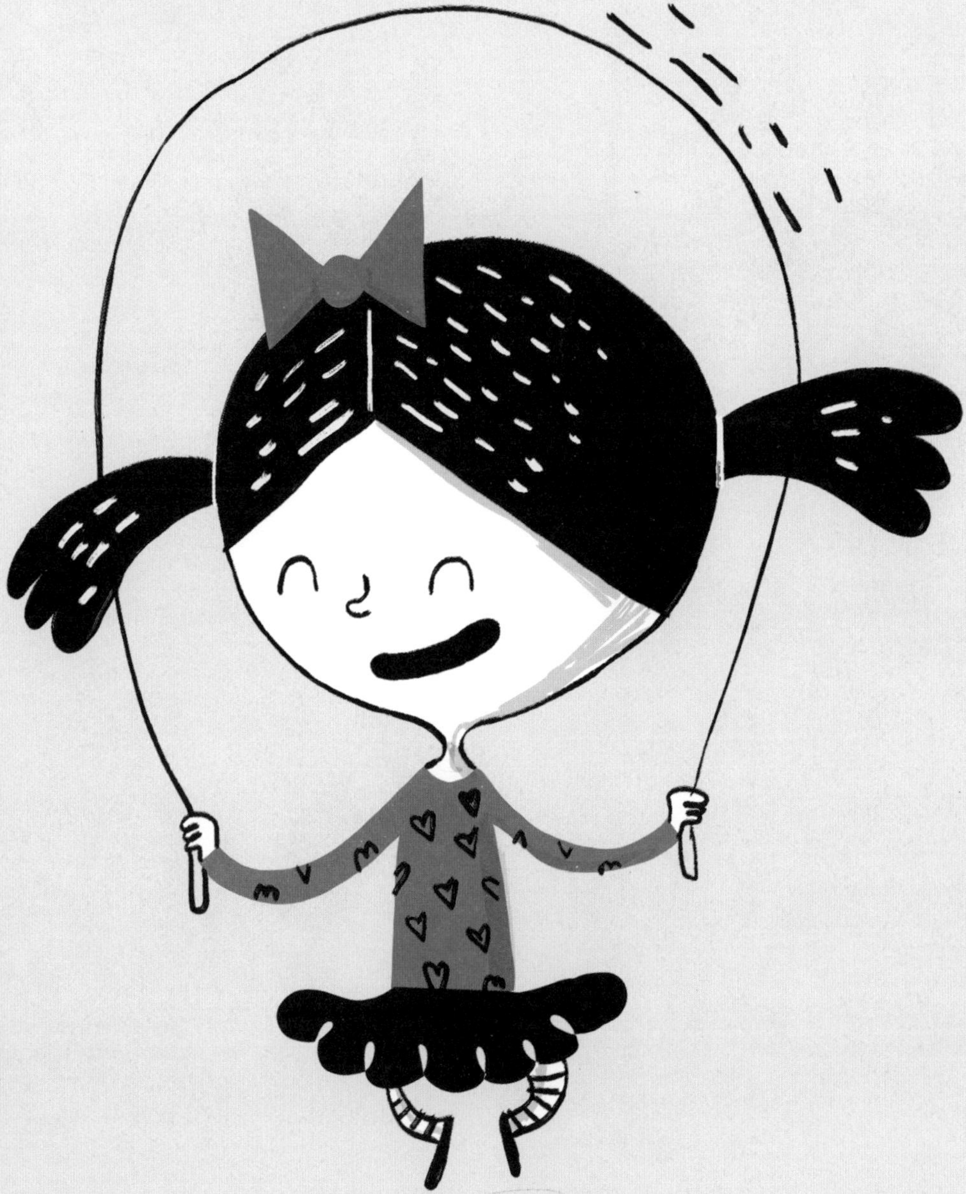

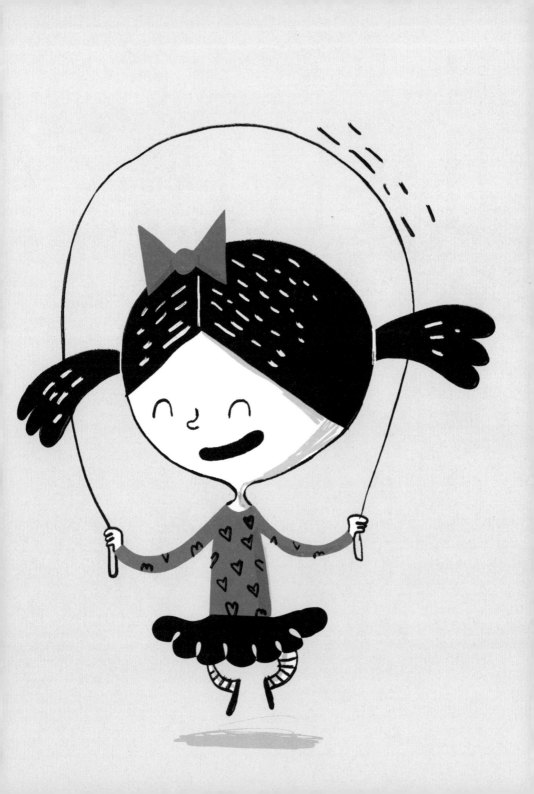

The spider can be helpful. Since she eats other

INSECTS,

she can get rid of annoying ones like mosquitoes and flies.

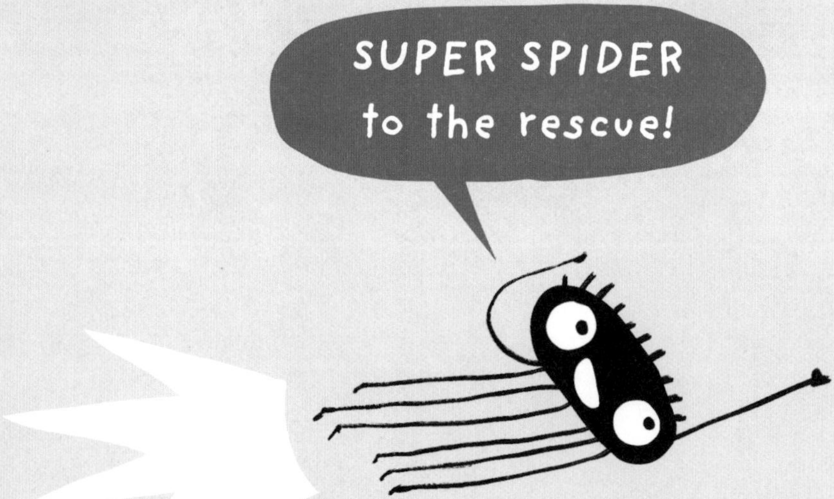
SUPER SPIDER
to the rescue!

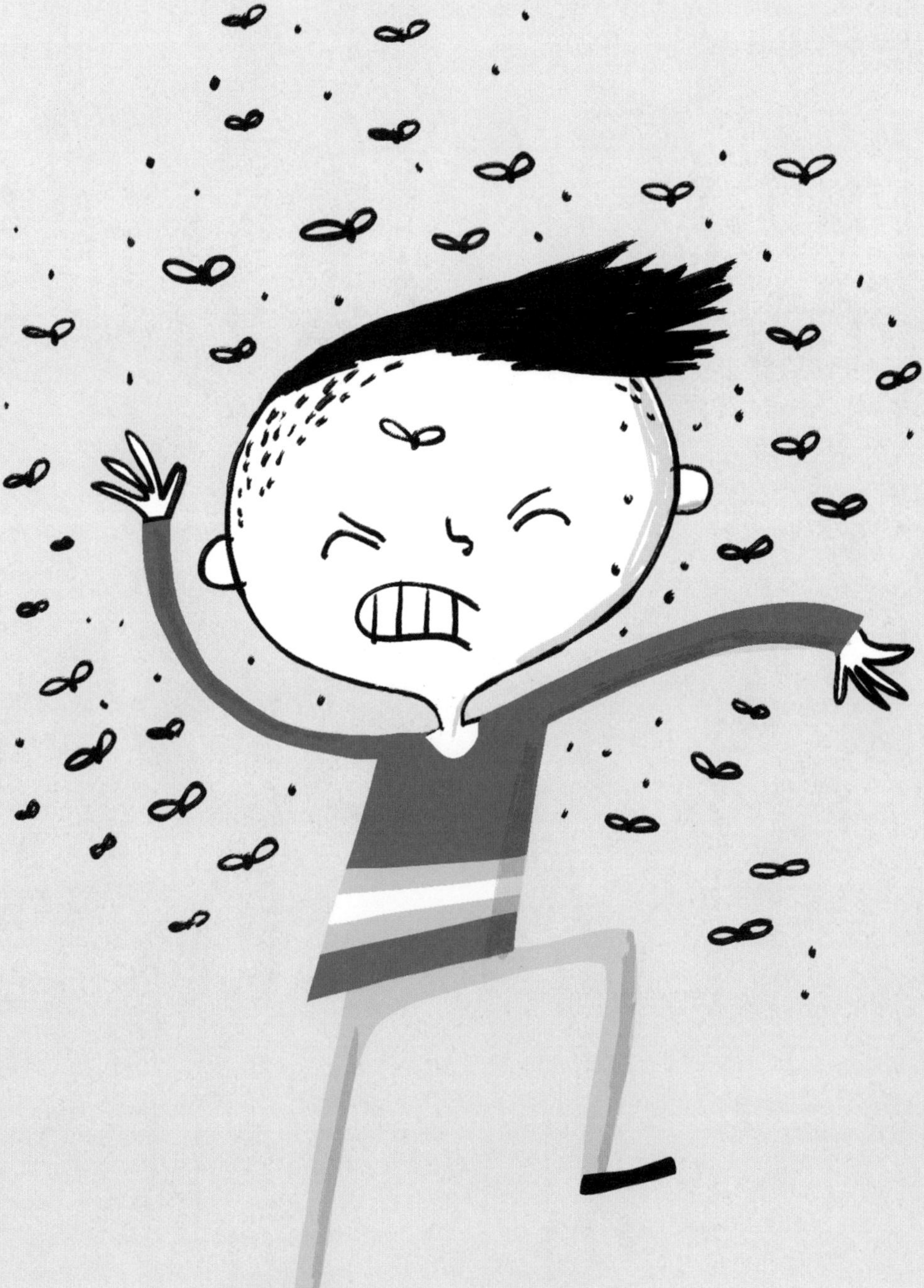

So the next time you meet a spider, shake her

HAND!

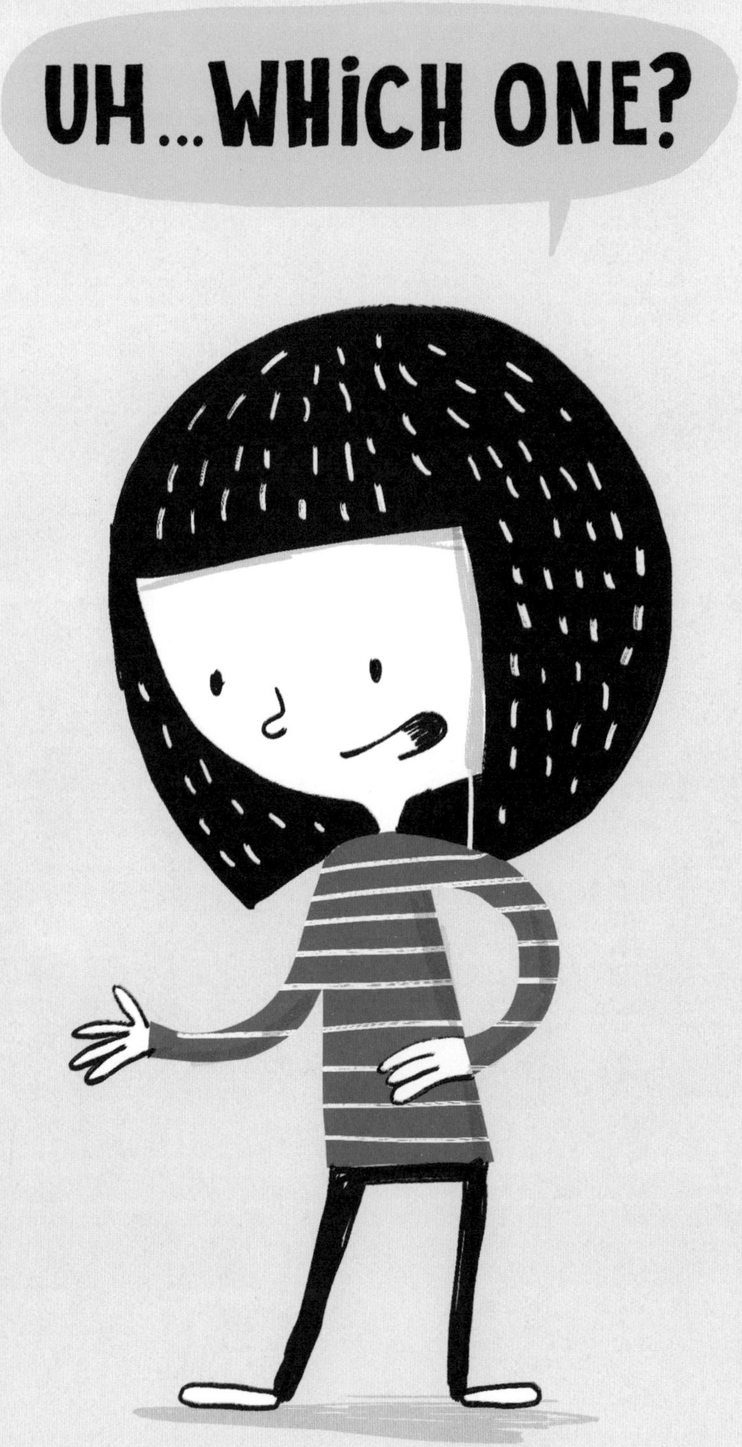
UH...WHICH ONE?

LOOK OUT FOR MORE

DISGUSTING CRITTERS

THE FLY

HELLO!

Elise Gravel

THE WORM

OH, HI!

Elise Gravel

THE RAT

HI!

Elise Gravel

THE SLUG

YO!

Elise Gravel

HEAD LICE

HEY THERE!

Elise Gravel

THE TOAD

Elise Gravel

GREETINGS!

THE COCKROACH

WELL HELLO!

Elise Gravel

THE BAT

WHATS UP?

Elise Gravel

THE MOSQUITO

Elise Gravel

HEYO!